A Gardener's Guide to Vegetables for Exhibition

By

G. T. Tinley

ALLOTMENT GARDENING
Preparation of the Ground—Manuring—Cropping—Fruits for Allotments—Monthly Operations—Vegetables as Food.

VEGETABLES FOR EXHIBITION

ALLOTMENT GARDENING

Soon after the declaration of war in August 1914 it was recognized that gardens could play an important part in providing food for the people. Their owners were therefore urged to grow vegetables at once wherever possible, and the following spring saw food-crops cultivated by nearly every one who had a garden, large or small. Much land which had hitherto been allowed to remain derelict or uncultivated was dug and cropped with Potatoes and other useful vegetables. The movement received a great stimulus from an Order under the Defence of the Realm Act, 1914, to extend the existing powers of acquiring suitable land for the growth of food vegetables.

Local authorities were authorized to do what was necessary to fit the land thus acquired for cultivation, including fencing; also to provide seeds, manures, and implements at cost price to the cultivators.

By July 1918 returns showed that there were no fewer than 1,400,000 allotments in the United Kingdom, occupying in England and Wales alone some 200,000 acres. These cultivated plots in evidence everywhere led to the remark that " the war turned Great Britain into an island of gardens."

Most of this war-time gardening has been undertaken by amateurs, and it is with the object of assisting them in the correct methods of allotment gardening that a special section is devoted to it here.

Large towns provided the greatest number of workers in this national scheme of gardening, and although land is more difficult to obtain in and near towns than in rural areas, the difficulty was to some extent surmounted by appropriating vacant building land and other derelict spaces, and by utilizing land in the public parks and gardens. Much of the ground consisted of old pasture, which had remained uncultivated for many years.

It is a popular fallacy that virgin soil, as waste land is popularly termed, will yield good crops without manure or dressing of any kind. It is true that old turf may contain a considerable amount of plant food, but it requires to be thoroughly broken up and decayed before this food is available. There is a danger also in digging virgin ground so deeply that the richer surface soil is buried out of the reach of the vegetables. Many failures in the first year of cultivating such ground are due to this cause.

Vegetables to be grown satisfactorily require, in addition to a supply of food at the roots, warmth, air, and moisture, and the operations of digging and manuring are, when properly performed, an aid to these requirements. Good digging means much in allotment gardening.

The most useful garden implement is the spade, and those who are skilled in its use will find that it is suitable for most ground operations. A small-bladed spade is better for amateurs unused to digging than one of large size. The fork is a valuable implement for breaking the hard subsoil, lifting root crops, loosening the surface soil, spreading manure, etc. Next to the spade and fork in usefulness comes the hoe, which is indispensable for the destruction of weeds, obtaining a fine tilth on the surface to prevent the soil from drying out rapidly in hot weather, making shallow drills for seeds, and earthing up Potatoes, etc. A rake is very serviceable for tidying ground and breaking down the lumps of soil when making a seed-bed. A garden line will ensure straight planting and should always be used in setting out crops. An iron-shod dibber is a handy implement for transplanting seedlings, and a trowel and hand fork will also be found of service.

PREPARATION OF THE GROUND

Soils vary so much that no hard and fast rules can be laid down for their treatment. They may be clayey, sandy, chalky, or peaty, the most fertile being those which contain a proportion of each of these materials, and are known as loams. The upper portion, known as the top soil, is that in which plants root and find nourishment; underneath this being the more close, solid strata, termed the subsoil. Where there is a good depth of rich upper soil the crops usually flourish, and one of the objects of tillage is to increase the depth of this fertile soil by breaking up the subsoil and incorporating with it manure, leaf-mould, vegetable refuse, wood-ash, road-sweepings, and in some cases lime. Some soils may be left undug until near the time for cropping, but others should be dug in the autumn and winter to receive the beneficial action of frost. Heavy soils consisting largely of clay, when well cultivated, usually prove the most productive. It is best not to cultivate such soils too deeply at first, but efforts should be made to provide good drainage, and any materials that will lighten ground, such as those mentioned above, should be dug in deeply in autumn and early winter. The soil should be thrown up in rough lumps so that the frosts, winds, sunshine and rain will act on it. Then, when spring arrives, it will fall to pieces easily and provide a suitable tilth for sowing and planting. Soot is an excellent dressing for heavy soil, and so is lime. The latter should be spread over the surface in late autumn and not dug in deeply, as it is washed down by rain. The effect of lime is to release the potash in clayey soils, to act as a sweetener by correcting acidity, and it is in itself a plant food. Two hundredweight of lime is a suitable dressing for a ten-rod plot. It should be slaked, which may be done by placing it in heaps and covering it with fine soil. Some soils are so heavy and wet that it is unwise to dig them much in advance of cropping. If disturbed in wet weather the surface becomes pasty and will take some time to recover. In digging any kind of soil take care not to bury it in big lumps which would remain throughout the growing season, for the roots of plants rarely or never enter clods. This precaution is necessary in ground intended for Potatoes, by far the most important crop grown on allotments.

Cow manure and pig manure are unsuited for heavy soils, as they make the soil heavier, colder, and more retentive of moisture. Avoid treading on heavy soil when it is wet, and do not wheel manure on it except when the surface is dry or frozen hard. There is a great variety of soils of medium texture, which with proper management may soon be brought into good condition. The free use of farmyard manure greatly improves such soil, and if the manure is applied in the autumn it will be well decayed by the spring, and should not cause forking in the roots of Parsnips and Carrots.

Light soils have certain advantages, being easy to work and warmer than those of a heavy texture. They have their disadvantages also, one of the chief being that they are not sufficiently retentive of moisture. Where the subsoil is clay, some of the latter should be brought up and mixed at the time of digging with the lighter surface soil. Sand is poor in plant foods, and it does not retain long anything that is added to enrich it. Clay, on the other hand, is very retentive of plant food, and it is to the absence of clay that the poorness of sandy soils is to be attributed. If either clay or marl—a term used for chalky loam—is applied in autumn or early winter it will greatly improve poor, light land. Light soils, being already in a fine state of division, do not require to be rough dug in autumn or early winter.

There are several ways of digging, namely: (1) ordinary digging; (2) forking; (3) trenching, *i.e.* turning over the soil to a depth of two or three feet; (4) bastard-trenching, or turning over the top spit only, and loosening the subsoil by forking and manuring; (5) ridging, or placing spadefuls of soil in rows so that they obtain the maximum of frost and air.

In ordinary digging it is best not to trust to the eye, however true, but to make use of the garden line: this will give a guide to the first spit, which should be dug to the full depth of the spade. When the first spit is turned over the soil below should be loosened with a fork. It is essential that the digging should be uniformly deep, partly because each trench has to be filled with the earth taken from the next one, and it is only by even digging that an even surface can be secured. When the first row is opened and

PREPARATION OF THE GROUND

the bottom loosened before the soil from the next row is turned on to it, manure of some kind should be put in. It will then serve the purpose of holding water, keeping it available for the thirsty plants in midsummer. Manure is not all of one kind; that from the stable and farmyard is best, but it is not always obtainable. The decayed leaves of the hedgerows are not to be despised, as they are a good water-holder and form humus by decay. Humus provides a medium in which fertilizing bacteria work and thrive. Good soil teems with them, and they enable the roots of plants to take up the nourishment it contains.

Trenching enables the roots to penetrate deeply and thus support the plants during drought. In trenching, first remove all the top soil from one end of the plot for about a yard in width, and place it near where the work is to finish. Then remove the subsoil, a spit deep, to the same spot. Now you have a trench two spits deep, with hard soil at the bottom. Fork this up, and lighten it with any suitable material, such as manure or horse-litter. The diagram on p. 199 will explain the process. If the plot is sufficiently wide another plan may be adopted to save carting soil to the opposite end. Stretch the garden line lengthways along the middle of the plot and trench one half at a time. As the work will finish at the same end as it was started from, only on the opposite side, the soil from the first trench is put there to fill in at the finish.

It is a great advantage when laying out land for allotments to make the plots of uniform size so that the pathways intersecting them are straight and of the same width. A common mistake is to make the paths too narrow and inconvenient for the use of wheelbarrows.

The verge or boundary of the plot should be a few inches away from the edge of the path, so that a narrow, shallow " V "-shaped trench is made. This cuts off the soil of the plot from that of the path, and has many advantages. Weeds from the grass path are not so likely to encroach on the cultivated ground, and it helps to keep the path dry.

The weeds as well as the old turf should be buried in digging, but there are certain weeds, such as Docks, Creeping Potentilla, Couch Grass and Bind Weed, which ought to be removed and burnt. The garden fire not only disposes of rubbish but it also provides in the ash a valuable fertilizer, Potash. Mixed with soot or lime, it is an excellent soil dressing. For example, seedling Turnips dressed with this mixture when the leaves are wet with the morning dews are protected from the ravages of the Turnip-fly. When a bonfire is properly made it will burn any kind of vegetable matter, however sappy and green it may be. To start the fire obtain a few stout sticks, such as old pea or bean sticks, and push them in the ground obliquely so that the tops meet in the centre. Arrange some dry fuel in the centre of these and cover the sticks with some of the driest material to be burnt. Light the fire on the windward side, and be ready to cover with fresh fuel any place where the flame breaks through. When the fire is going well it will burn almost anything combustible. The ash should be collected and stored in the dry for use in spring. It is an excellent fertilizer for Potatoes if sprinkled on the soil before the seed Potatoes are put in. Another use of the garden bonfire is to destroy garden pests, both insect and fungoid. The spores and mycelium of disease hibernate in old and decaying vegetation, and become active again in the spring. The eggs of many insect pests which are attached to old vegetation are destroyed in the same way.

MANURING

The chemical constituents of the food of plants are carbon, oxygen, hydrogen, nitrogen, sulphur, iron, phosphorus, potash, magnesium, and calcium. For the last seven of these we must look to the soil; and if only one of these chemicals is absent or insufficient the plant is handicapped, although it may possess abundance of all the rest. There is, as a rule, no dearth of iron in the soil. It is this which colours brown the clays and sands of this country. Plants do not need much iron, and they generally find all they want. Calcium in the form of chalk or lime also is present in most soils, but no harm is done by adding more, calcium being an important constituent. Sulphur compounds exist plentifully in nature, so that we need not concern ourselves particularly with these. Nor is magnesium likely to be lacking. The three most important are nitrogen, phosphorus, and potash, and the quantity of these three chemicals in the soil regulates the growth of the plant. The whole object of manuring is to provide an adequate supply of them. All three may be present in other things besides animal manure, but dung is the best fertilizer, because it contains all the necessary plant foods as well as humus which the straw provides. Nitrogen is present in leaf-mould and other forms of decaying vegetable matter; also in hair, hoof, horn, blood, fish refuse, soot, seaweed, and poultry droppings. Phosphorus is contained in guano and bones; and potash in wood-ash, the flue-dust from blast furnaces, and in seaweed. Offal from the fishmonger mixed with dry soil and left in a heap until it is decayed is a good plant manure. Sweepings from the bootmaker's shop and hoof parings from the forge contain a considerable quantity of nitrogen. Soot from chimneys and flues should be collected and kept dry for use in spring. Sulphate of ammonia and nitrate of soda supply nitrogen; superphosphate, bone meal and basic slag, phosphorus; kainit or muriate of potash, potash. Bone meal and basic slag are two useful phosphatic fertilizers. Basic slag is slow-acting and should be applied to the ground in autumn at the rate of 4 oz. to the square yard.

Carbon, an important plant food, is obtained from the atmosphere. Green leaves assimilate carbon under the influence of sunlight. This is why most plants must be allowed plenty of sunshine and fresh air.

The best time to apply farmyard manure is the autumn, for then it will be thoroughly decayed by the spring and ready for the plants to make use of, the foods it contains enabling them to make good growth at the start, which is important. Fresh dung, often spoken of by professional gardeners as poisonous to plants, is of no use to them until it has decayed. If used in spring and summer it is best placed on the surface as a mulch, where its manurial properties will be washed down by the rains to the roots, the litter serving to prevent evaporation of soil moisture in dry weather. Quick-acting manures that are readily soluble, such as nitrate of soda, should only be used for growing plants.

A good substitute for farmyard manure is leaf-mould, made from the leaves of beech, oak, and other trees. Where trees are plentiful there is usually an accumulation of leaf-mould to be found beneath them, and in woods of long standing it sometimes forms a deep layer of rich vegetable mould. In addition to the plant foods contained in dead leaves or leaf-mould, it serves to lighten heavy soils and adds body to light ones.

Where seaweed can be obtained easily it well repays to collect it for the garden. Seaweed may be dug in during the autumn similar to stable manure, or it may be placed in a heap and mixed with lime and soil to form when rotted a compost for use as a top-dressing, or as a substitute for farmyard manure. Rotted seaweed is good as a top-dressing for asparagus and sea-kale. It contains a considerable amount of potash, and is on that account recommended as a manure for Potatoes. Road-sweepings containing horse-droppings and free from oil or tar, if stored for a time and turned frequently to allow the air to sweeten them, are good to mix with heavy soils.

Poultry- and pigeon-dung contains nitrogen and phosphorus. The droppings should be dried and mixed with fine soil before use. Both pig and cow manures are good for light soils, as they serve to retain moisture in the ground in summer. These manures are best when plenty of straw is mixed with them, as it helps to keep the soil open. Fresh horse-dung should be mixed with dead leaves or some such littery material, or fibrous turf that has been stacked for about twelve months may be mixed with it, as it will absorb the ammonia and increase the bulk. Manure water is probably the least expensive and most easily obtained fertilizer, as well as one of the best. It may be applied to all growing crops. It is easily stored in a barrel or a galvanized dustbin with a tight-fitting lid. The manure should consist mainly of horse- and cow-droppings and soot which can be tied in a piece of sacking and dropped into the water. The liquid should be about the colour of pale beer when used. Soot alone tied in a piece of sacking and placed in the tub of water can be used in the same way.

The rules to be observed in applying concentrated fertilizers are: lime, basic slag, bone meal, superphosphate, and kainit should be applied on the surface and lightly forked in.

Sulphate of ammonia, nitrate of soda, sulphate of potash, and guano should be spread on the surface to be washed in by the rain. Lime should not be mixed with manures but used alone. Basic slag contains a lot of free lime, and should also be used alone. Superphosphate of lime should be applied to light soils in the spring, but basic slag is best applied in the autumn.

Different manures have different effects on crops. Stable manure, although good for all crops, can be used in excess. This is also true of chemical fertilizers.

CROPPING

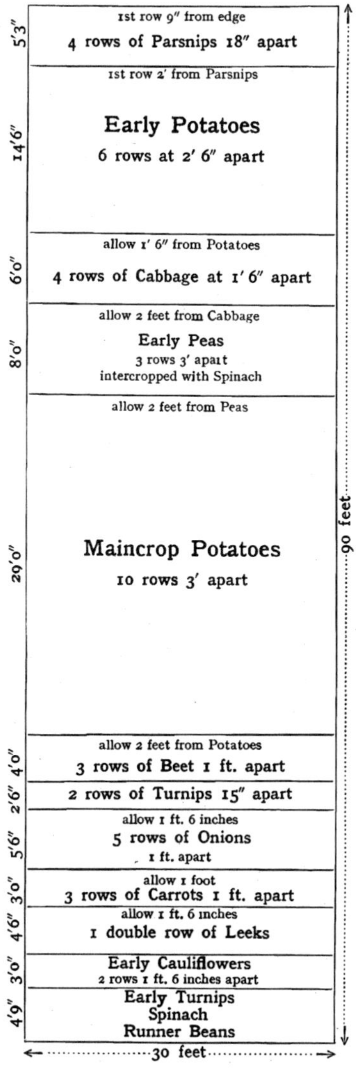

A ten-rod plot is a convenient size for an amateur to cultivate in his spare time, and if properly managed it should provide a supply of useful vegetables all the year round. The most serviceable crops are Potatoes, Parsnips, Carrots, Turnips, Jerusalem Artichokes, Beet, Onions, Leeks, Dwarf Beans, Runner Beans, and the various members of the Cabbage family, including Cauliflowers, Broccoli, Brussels Sprouts, Kales, and Savoys. Next in value come Broad Beans, Peas, Celery, Shallots, Spinach, Endive, and Sea-kale. Outdoor Tomatoes do very well in some seasons, and if all the fruits do not ripen the green ones may be used for making jam or chutney. Marrows and Gourds are easily grown, though their food value is not great, and they occupy a considerable amount of ground. Lettuces, Radishes, and Mustard and Cress are easily grown and are good as salads.

A cold frame is a good investment, and one of the best uses to which it can be put in summer is to grow Frame Cucumbers. In the late winter and spring it will be found invaluable for raising an early crop of Radishes and seedlings for transplanting in the open. In winter it may be utilised for protecting seedling Cauliflowers, Endive, Lettuces, and Parsley. A two-light frame is also handy for holding the various tools, which will occupy only a little space along the front. It is essential to keep tools with wooden handles in the dry, as exposure to the weather causes the handles to crack and splinter and the iron parts to rust.

For the novice it is better to attempt the cultivation of a few things well the first season; and a start might be made with Parsnips, Potatoes, Onions, Carrots, Turnips, and various green crops. No vegetable is better for a first crop on newly turned soil than Potatoes, and at least one-half of the plot should be cropped with them. The reason why the soil is improved when this crop is grown is because of the number of times it is turned. Weeds seldom trouble Potatoes, because the soil is so frequently disturbed, whilst in summer the haulm grows so thick and dense as to entirely smother any weeds that may spring up beneath it.

In all systems of cropping care must be taken not to plant a tall-growing vegetable too near a dwarf-growing kind. For example, Potatoes should not be put close to rows of Carrots and Beet, as the haulms might fall over and smother their neighbours.

A moderately tall growing crop, such as Cabbages, which can well look after them-

Fig. 200.—Method of cropping a ten-rod plot (90 feet × 30 feet). Winter Green Crops may follow Early Peas; and Celery Early Potatoes. Late Turnips can succeed Cabbages.

Plot layout (90 feet × 30 feet):

- 1st row 9" from edge
- 4 rows of Parsnips 18" apart
- 1st row 2' from Parsnips
- **Early Potatoes** — 6 rows at 2' 6" apart
- allow 1' 6" from Potatoes
- 4 rows of Cabbage at 1' 6" apart
- allow 2 feet from Cabbage
- **Early Peas** — 3 rows 3' apart, intercropped with Spinach
- allow 2 feet from Peas
- **Maincrop Potatoes** — 10 rows 3' apart
- allow 2 feet from Potatoes
- 3 rows of Beet 1 ft. apart
- 2 rows of Turnips 15" apart
- allow 1 ft. 6 inches
- 5 rows of Onions 1 ft. apart
- allow 1 foot
- 3 rows of Carrots 1 ft. apart
- allow 1 ft. 6 inches
- 1 double row of Leeks
- **Early Cauliflowers** — 2 rows 1 ft. 6 inches apart
- **Early Turnips**
- **Spinach**
- **Runner Beans**

selves, would be much better. Nor should tall Beans be put next to Tomatoes, for the one would obstruct the light from the other. Some crops require better soil than others, and in any cropping plan this must be considered. Onions should be given the best piece of ground, whereas Turnips will succeed almost anywhere, their chief requirement being plenty of moisture.

Jerusalem Artichoke is not particular in its soil requirements, and is often grown in headlands and waste spaces. Deep-growing root crops, such as Parsnips and Carrots, require a good depth of fine soil that was well manured for a previous crop. For Leeks and Celery it is necessary to make trenches and work a good layer of stable manure into the bottom, with enough soil on the top in which to plant the seedlings.

This plan of growing crops in trenches with dung at the bottom is also followed very successfully with Peas and Runner Beans. All such crops require plenty of moisture in summer, and the value of the dung at the bottom of the roots is not so much to feed the plants as to hold moisture and provide a damp medium for the roots.

Where the ground has been dug in autumn or winter and is ready for cropping by the time the new year arrives a start may be made in February with the sowing of Parsnips, Broad Beans, and early Peas. Jerusalem Artichokes may also be planted in February, and if these four are got in early in the year it will leave less to be done when the busy time of March and April arrives. It is not too soon in February to sow in a cold frame early Lettuces, summer Cabbages, Onions, Leeks, early Cauliflowers and Brussels Sprouts. The grower should endeavour to adopt a system of cropping whereby a crop follows on as soon as one is cleared.

The first crops to be harvested are Spinach, Turnips, early Potatoes, Shallots, early Peas, and Broad Beans, and when these are cleared in early July they may be succeeded by Celery, Turnips, Kohl-rabi, Brussels Sprouts, Savoys, Cauliflowers, and other green crops; shorthorn Carrots, Beet, Endive, and Lettuce.

The garden year may start in almost any month, but in many respects February is the best time for an amateur to commence garden operations other than those of digging. In this month the days begin to lengthen, spring is approaching and winter is almost over, making the cultivator long to get to work again. Even if all the plot is not dug by February a start may be made with seed sowing and, as the season advances, the ground will get drier and digging operations become easier. Of course March is the great month for seed sowing, and while it is well to get the crops in early, it is a mistake to sow on land that is cold and wet; it is much better to defer sowing until the ground is in a friable condition, even if it entails waiting a whole month or more.

Parsnips planted in May have been known to give almost as good results as those sown in February, and the same is true with regard to Potatoes; it is better to plant them late in soil that is dry and warm, than to plant early in cold, water-logged soil.

A garden-line should always be used when making rows for planting seeds. The line should be stretched tightly and rest just level with the surface; the hoe is the best implement for making the drills, and the foot should be placed on the line as the hoe is drawn close to it. For small seeds draw a drill about an inch deep in order to allow a covering of fine soil to protect the seeds from birds. Carrots, Turnips, Radishes, Lettuces, and Cabbages should be sown at this depth, but for Broad Beans, Runner Beans, Peas, and Dwarf and Haricot Beans a depth of 3 or 4 inches is necessary. It is best to sow thinly using reliable seeds, which are always the most economical in the end, if a little dearer to purchase, thin sowing meaning a saving of labour in thinning the seedlings. Large seeds are best placed in twos or threes at the proper distance apart. For Parsnips it is a good plan to hold a few seeds in the left hand and with the finger and thumb of the right hand pick out two or three and place them where a Parsnip will occupy the space, repeating this every 6 or 8 inches along the line. It will be an easy matter to draw out the one or two surplus seedlings from each group when they are up. Thinning should always be done early, as when plants are crowded they grow tall and impoverish each other. Sturdy, stocky growth is always best, as it indicates vigour and robustness, and the plants have a good start. It is a common mistake of amateurs to attempt to grow too many plants in a given area by crowding them in the rows and not allowing sufficient space between the rows themselves. It may appear too much space to give the room advised by experts when the ground is clear and the seeds are being sown, but if the crops are to succeed they must have room when they are full grown; moreover, space will be needed to permit of such operations as hoeing and weeding. The distances advised below for planting the various crops

CROPPING

are the minimum to allow, and those who desire extra fine produce would be well advised to err on the side of more rather than less space.

As soon as the seeds are sown, the surface should be made level and, unless the soil is very moist, the ground along the rows made firm by treading. Most seeds germinate best in firm ground mainly because the particles of soil hold moisture longer when they are close together. It is a well-known fact that corn comes up best and strongest in the ruts where carts have passed along the field, and where depressions are made by horses' hoofs as the hunters pass over the fields in early spring. For some crops, Onions for example, it is essential to make the soil quite firm, the usual practice being to tread it well. This should be done when the soil is dry and friable on the surface, otherwise the treading would cause it to cake, and seeds need air as well as moisture and warmth to germinate. Birds greedily eat the seedlings of some vegetables, and others are subject to the attacks of insects, such as the Turnip-fly and Onion-fly. Dusting the rows with a mixture of wood-ash and lime or soot is one of the best methods of deterring both birds and insects from attacking seedlings. The dusting should be done when the leaves are wet with dew in the early morning or after a shower. Besides serving as a protection these materials stimulate growth; as the plants get older they are less susceptible to attack.

Certain vegetables, such as Onions, all the members of the Cabbage family, Leeks, Celery, Lettuces, Endive, Peas, Beans of all sorts, and Parsley transplant with ease, but others, such as Parsnips and Turnips, Beet and Carrots, are seldom a success when transplanted. The best time for transplanting is in showery weather, and late in the day rather than early, as the plants then get the benefit of the night dews, which assists them to recover quickly, and they will be less liable to droop and wither. Large seedlings, if set with a dibber, require that the hole should be made and filled with water before the roots are inserted, first allowing the water to drain away, otherwise the soil would be so pasty that it would be impossible to make it sufficiently firm about the roots. A good watering after the plants are set is a great advantage, and if the weather is dry it may be necessary to give other waterings to enable the roots to become established.

The following table shows the time for sowing and planting for successional cropping, with the distances at which the various crops should be set.

VARIETIES OF VEGETABLES SUITABLE FOR ALLOTMENTS

BEET. — Improved Globe, Crimson Globe, Blood Red, Dell's Crimson, Nutting's Dark Red.
BROAD BEANS.—Green Windsor, Mammoth Long Pod and Prolific Long Pod.
BORECOLE or KALE.—Cottager's Kale, Tall Green, Green-curled Dwarf.
BRUSSELS SPROUTS.—Scrymger's Giant Exhibition, Paris Market, and The Wroxton.
CABBAGE.—Early varieties: Ellam's Early, Harbinger, April, and Flower of Spring. Main crop varieties: Enfield Market, Wheeler's Imperial, Offenham.
BROCCOLI.—Walcheren, Perfection, Veitch's Self-Protecting, Early Purple Sprouting.
CARROTS.—Early Scarlet Horn, Scarlet Intermediate, Early Nantes, James's Intermediate, and Long Red Surrey.
CAULIFLOWERS.—Early Autumn Giant, Early London, Veitch's Autumn Giant, Snowball.
CELERY.—Sandringham White, Giant White, Aldenham Red and Solid Red.
ENDIVE.—Batavian, Moss Curled.
LETTUCE.—Paris White (Cos), All the Year Round (Cabbage).
LEEKS.—Musselburgh, the Lyon and Prizetaker.
VEGETABLE MARROW.—Long White Trailing, Long Green, Pen-y-byd.
ONIONS.—Ailsa Craig, James's Long Keeping, Nuneham Park, Prizetaker, Bedfordshire Champion.
PARSLEY.—Giant Curled, Myatt's Garnishing.
PARSNIPS.—Hollow Crown, Student, Large Guernsey.
PEAS.—Chelsea Gem, Little Marvel, English Wonder, Gradus, Chelsea Prolific, Duke of Albany, and Autocrat.
RADISH.—French Breakfast and Scarlet Globe.
SPINACH.—Victoria, Improved Round, New Zealand, and Perpetual or Spinach Beet.
TOMATOES.—Ailsa Craig, Sunrise, and Lister's Prolific.
TURNIPS.—Red Globe, White Stone, Greentop Stone, Golden Ball, and Garden Swede.
POTATOES.—Early: Duke of York, Midlothian Early, Myatt's Ash Leaf. Second early: Windsor Castle, British Queen. Main crop: King Edward, Arran Chief, Up-to-date, the Factor.

ALLOTMENT GARDENING

FRUITS FOR ALLOTMENTS

The most suitable kinds of fruit for cultivating on allotments are Strawberries, Raspberries, Red, White, and Black Currants, Gooseberries, Loganberries, and Cut-leaved Blackberry.

Strawberry layers need to be specially prepared and planted early to fruit the first season. The best are from plants which have been forced into fruit early in the same year, but these are rather difficult to obtain. The next best plants are those specially rooted in small pots. The soil for Strawberries should be dug deeply, and enriched with well-rotted manure. They should be set in rows 2 feet apart and 18 inches between; some growers set them 1 foot apart in the rows and move every alternate plant in the second year. Royal Sovereign, King George, and Givon's Late Prolific are first-class varieties.

Raspberries to obtain a quick crop should be planted in late autumn leaving the canes their full length and cutting down every alternate plant to within 1 foot of the ground. The uncut canes should fruit the following season, whilst the others will develop strong suckers for the next year. The old canes should be removed directly the fruit has been gathered to enable plenty of sunlight and air to reach the shoots of the current season and cause them to become firm and ripe. The rows should be 3 feet apart and the crowns 1 foot apart in the rows.

The Red Currant and the White Currant are varieties of the same species, and they both require to be pruned to very short spurs, at the base of which the fruiting buds develop in clusters. It is best to grow these plants with a stem as the ground can then be better kept clear of weeds. The Black Currant, on the contrary, fruits on the new wood, and in order to obtain plenty of young basal shoots the lower eyes are not removed when the cuttings are rooted, so that the plants continue to send up sucker shoots. In pruning the Black Currant most of the old useless wood should be removed each season after fruiting, but the young wood should be left. The Gooseberry is one of the easiest fruits to cultivate, and may generally be relied upon to crop well. The fruits develop on both the old and the new wood, therefore the only pruning that is necessary is to remove all suckers and such shoots as are needed to prevent overcrowding, keeping the centre of the bush open to allow the air and sunshine to enter freely and facilitate the gathering of the berries. The Loganberry and other members of the Bramble family, such as the Lowberry and the Cut-leaved Bramble, send out strong, sucker-like shoots—in the case of the Loganberry sometimes 20 feet long—and if the wood is well ripened the plants will fruit well every year. The old fruiting stems should be cut out, as in the case of the Raspberry, to which these brambles are allied, directly after the berries are gathered.

The Sutton is one of the finest of all varieties of Rhubarb, other good sorts being Daw's Champion and Champagne. The crowns should be planted in deeply dug ground, to which plenty of well-rotted manure has been added.

MONTHLY OPERATIONS

January.—During this month the soil is generally either too wet or too hard with frost to permit of ground operations, but whenever it is sufficiently dry digging should be proceeded with to get as much of it as possible ready for planting and sowing later. Towards the end of the month Broad Beans may be sown for transplanting in March; where frames are available Broad Beans, early Peas, early Cabbage and Lettuce should be sown in them for transplanting in the open in April. On a very sheltered, warm border sow early Peas, a round-seeded sort for preference. When the ground is hard with frost wheel manure on to the plot. Look over Spring Cabbages and where any of the plants have failed replace them with others from the seed-bed; this should be done in mild weather when the ground is fairly dry.

February.—The same crops as recommended for planting and sowing in January may be put in, and Jerusalem Artichokes and Shallots planted. Towards the end of the month a sowing of Peas may be made on land that is moderately dry, wet soil being bad for early Peas. Towards the end of the month Spinach and Parsnip seed may be got in. Sow early Cauliflowers, Leeks, and Brussels Sprouts in frames.

March.—Sow Shorthorn Carrots, Lettuce, summer Cabbage, Turnips, Spinach, early

MONTHLY OPERATIONS

Peas, Broad Beans, and Parsnips. Towards the end of the month make a sowing out-of-doors of Lettuce, Brussels Sprouts, Parsley, Leeks, Snow's Winter White and Late Queen Broccoli, early London and Autumn Giant Cauliflowers, Onions and Radishes. Sow Celery, Onions, and Leeks in frames. A few early Potatoes may be planted in a warm situation. They may need a little protection if they come through when the weather is frosty.

April.—Continue to plant the crops recommended for March, and towards the end of the month make the first sowing of Beet and French Beans. Finish the planting of early Potatoes and, as the season advances, put in the second earlies and follow with the main crop sorts. Raise Marrows and Cucumbers in warm frames, and in the second fortnight of the month sow Savoys, Curled Greens (Kales), early and late Cauliflowers, and further sowing of Turnips, Peas, Onions, Carrots, and Brussels Sprouts.

May.—Continue to make successional sowings of Beet, Spinach, Carrots, Lettuce, Peas, Radishes, late Broccoli and Kales. Plant out early Leeks, Brussels Sprouts, and Cauliflowers. After the 20th of the month it will be safe to plant Tomatoes out-of-doors. Mustard and Cress will make good progress; they need plenty of moisture, and must be watered in dry weather. Scarlet Runners should be sown during the first week of the month; seedlings raised in boxes in frames should be set out, and staked immediately they are planted.

June.—Continue to sow Dwarf and Runner Beans and make the final sowing of Broad Beans. Transplant the various members of the Cabbage family before they become too large. Make trenches for Celery and Leeks as soon as space used for early Peas and Potatoes is available. In hot weather Turnips, Lettuces, Radishes, and other moisture-loving crops should be sown on a cool border. It will be better to thin Lettuces now than to transplant them. Pull up surplus plants from the rows of Onions and use them as salad.

July.—As soon as early Peas, Beans, and Potatoes have been gathered prepare the ground for Celery, winter Greens, and Cauliflowers. Plant the main crop of Broccoli and sow prickly seeded Spinach to stand through the winter. Of root crops choose the early sorts such as Shorthorn Carrots, Globe Beet, and early White Stone Turnip. Put in a little Parsley seed and thin the plants when they are large enough to handle at 6 inches apart. Remove all the side-shoots from Tomatoes and stake the plants securely.

August.—Make a sowing of Onions about the third week to obtain plants for transplanting in spring. In the first or second week sow seed of spring Cabbages such as Flower of Spring, Ellam's Early, Harbinger, and April. A small sowing of Cabbage may be made at the same time. Sow a hardy dwarf Cabbage Lettuce, Hammersmith or Bath Cos, to stand the winter. Sow winter Spinach and make a final sowing of Turnips. More Celery should be planted early in the month.

September.—Plant vacant ground with all kinds of winter Greens. Endeavour to lift all Potatoes by the end of the month as the ground may get over wet in October and cause many of the tubers to contract disease. Onions should be harvested and dried thoroughly before they are placed in store. Assist the ripening of Tomatoes by removing the foliage where it shades the fruit. Late Cauliflowers should be lifted and transferred to frames where they will receive protection during cold weather. Earth up Celery and Leeks when the soil is in a workable condition.

October.—In fine weather the planting of green crops may be continued. Hardy Lettuces may be pricked out in rows, making the soil firm about the roots. Lift Carrots and Beet before the roots crack through excessive moisture in the soil, and store them in ashes or dry soil under a dry wall. Make a general clearance of the remains of all crops that are finished, burn the rubbish, and get as much of the ground dug as possible before it becomes too wet with autumn rains.

November.—Make Asparagus beds tidy by removing all weeds and rubbish, and apply a surface dressing of rich soil containing plenty of manure. A portion of such hardy crops as Jerusalem Artichokes, Parsnips, and Celery should be lifted when the ground is free from frost, as there may be times when it will be impossible to do this. See that the green crops are not loosened by the action of frost, treading the soil firmly wherever necessary. Clear away all dead leaves from the various greens and keep the crops clear of weeds, to allow the air to circulate freely about the plants.

Endeavour to complete the digging and trenching of all vacant ground so that the soil may receive the beneficial influence of frost.

December.—Whenever the ground is in a suitable condition proceed with tillage operations, as it is an advantage to have

ALLOTMENT GARDENING

a considerable area of the plot ready for sowing and planting when the New Year arrives. Straighten the path margins and get the plot as neat and tidy as possible. Prepare stakes, etc., for future use. Think out a plan of operations, selecting the kinds of seeds to be grown and the positions for each, bearing in mind that a change of position is good for all kinds. Arrange Potatoes intended for sets in boxes and place them in a frost-proof shed, where they will be exposed to light.

VEGETABLES AS FOOD

The following lists give the commoner vegetables in the order in which they possess nutrient solids. The most useful varieties to grow for food are thus indicated; in selecting any vegetable, however, the allotment-holder should bear in mind the relative facility of its cultivation, the nature of the soil, and other factors.

The numbers are percentages of nutrient solids, the balance being water. The chief constituents are indicated by the letters M (Mineral Salts), C (Carbohydrates), P (Proteins), and F (Fat).

PULSES

1. Broad Beans (dry) .... 91.6 MCPF
2. Peas .... 21.9 MCP
3. French Beans .... 10.5 MC
4. Scarlet Runners (stewed) ... 8.9 C

ROOTS AND TUBERS

1. Potatoes .... 21.7 MCP
2. Artichokes (Jerusalem) .... 20.2 MCPF
3. Parsnips .... 19.9 MCPF
4. Beetroots .... 16.1 MC
5. Carrots .... 14.3 MCF
6. Turnips .... 9.7 MC
7. Radishes .... 9.2 MCP

OTHER VEGETABLES

1. Kale (Borecole) .... 17.1 MCPF
2. Savoys .... 13.0 MC
3. Onions .... 10.9 MPF
4. Cabbage .... 10.4 MCPF
5. Red Cabbage .... 10.0 MCP
6. Cauliflower .... 9.3 MCPF
7. Leeks .... 8.2 MCPF
8. Tomatoes .... 8.1 MCP
9. Celery .... 6.6 MCP
10. Brussels Sprouts .... 6.3 MCP
11. Lettuce .... 5.9 MCPF
12. Rhubarb .... 5.4 CF
13. Vegetable Marrow .... 5.2 C

VITAMINES

Vitamines are chemical compounds, but little is known of their composition; they are helpful, as they act upon the food previous to or during actual digestion and are thus "intermediate agents" in the digestive processes. They are easily destroyed and therefore easily removed in food preparation. Their absence from food-stuffs is in some way connected with the occurrence of certain diseases—*e.g.* beri-beri and, probably, scurvy. Generally they occur only in minute quantities; but in some food-stuffs—and often in special portions thereof—they are more abundant: *e.g.* in fresh vegetables and in fruit juices; the husk of rice, wheat, and other cereals; the brain and heart of mammals and birds; and in the eggs of birds and in yeasts.

TURNIPS are fleshy roots which contain more water than milk does, only 5 per cent of carbohydrates, and no starch. As a food they are therefore unimportant. The "Swede" is somewhat more nutritious than the usual white variety.

JERUSALEM ARTICHOKES are tubers which contain no starch, but a fair proportion of other carbohydrates, the effect of which is to make the cooked vegetable mucilaginous. Great loss of nutrient substances may occur in cooking; this may be obviated by steaming them in their skins.

POTATOES are an important article of diet, rich in starch. The constituents are distributed very variously in the different parts: the outside layer immediately beneath the brown skin contains most protein, fat, and mineral matter; the flesh contains the most starch; and a narrow, intermediate layer the most water with some protein and mineral matter.

Dextrin and "British" arrowroot are prepared from Potato starch; and Potatoes are also employed in the making of bread with wheat flour. They cannot, however, be regarded as a complete substitute for bread, because they are too bulky a food, and they contain too little protein in proportion to starch.

The method of cooking any vegetable—especially tubers—is all-important. Potatoes should always be steamed or cooked in their "jackets"; they should not be boiled, especially after peeling. Potatoes which are "waxy" when cooked are richer in protein; this is characteristic of "new" Potatoes. The floury varieties are the more digestible.

It has been calculated that if 16 lbs. of

VEGETABLES AS FOOD

Potatoes were peeled and soaked before being boiled, the loss of nutrients would be nearly equivalent to the amount contained in $\frac{1}{4}$ lb. of beefsteak.

BEETROOT.—A fleshy root containing a large amount of sugar. Unless great care is taken not to bruise or break the skin, a large proportion of the sugar is lost in cooking. Beetroot is fairly rich in cellulose—and this is rendered softer and more digestible when vinegar is added.

CARROTS are fleshy roots which owe their nutritious value mainly to the sugar they contain; they also contain protein and some quantity of available mineral matter. Hence, although not very digestible, they are a useful food.

PARSNIPS are fleshy roots having 14 per cent of carbohydrates chiefly in the form of starch and sugar; the loss on cooking when peeled bringing the percentage down to 1.4.

GREEN VEGETABLES have a very low nutritive value, but they are of great importance in diet for several reasons. They supply material which acts as a stimulus to the alimentary canal. The mineral matter they contain is largely alkaline and tends to check acidity; and the iron in them is an important source of that substance in the diet. The vitamines are strongly represented; and it is probable that the presence of these constituents largely accounts for the curative powers and wholesomeness of green vegetables. Their poorness in fat leads to their common use with butter, oil, or dripping. Green vegetables are not easily digested or absorbed. They should be eaten as fresh as possible, as otherwise they may set up fermentation. Some, however, may be preserved. CABBAGES contain 89 per cent of water. CAULIFLOWER is the most easily digested. SCARLET RUNNERS and FRENCH BEANS contain much carbohydrate in the form of cellulose—which makes them digested and absorbed with difficulty.

RHUBARB.—A valuable vegetable food, containing a fair amount of carbohydrate, cellulose, and mineral matter.

ONIONS.—An Onion is a bulb, *i.e.* a collection of swollen, overlapping scales completely concealing the central disc-like stem. The oil they contain makes them useful for flavouring. The Spanish Onion is rather more nutritious than the other varieties.

PEAS, BEANS, and LENTILS.—The characteristic food constituent of the Pulses is protein, hence their name of " the poor man's beef "; they also have a high percentage of carbohydrate. It is owing to this latter fact that we often find them served with fat-containing foods, *e.g.* pork with pease pudding, bacon with beans.

These foods are highly nutritious. They are slowly digested and very completely absorbed. They are amongst the cheapest of foods, but their poorness in fat necessitates this being supplied from other foods.

As usual with the cooking of vegetables, attention should be paid to details. Dried Peas and Beans should be well soaked with the special object of softening the skins, although this results in some loss of the food-constituents. Hard water should not be used for soaking or cooking. Soft water or boiled water should be used for soaking; or ordinary washing-soda may be added to the water for either purpose.

GREEN PEAS contain a certain amount of their carbohydrate in the form of sugar.

BEANS in general contain more protein than Peas.

LENTILS are still richer in protein—the small varieties being the best; and iron is an important mineral constituent. They are more easily digested than Peas or Beans. Lentils are also used in the form of lentil flour.

FRESH FRUITS.—Considered as articles of food, fruits may be regarded as fruits for flavouring, food fruits, and, to a limited extent, as substitutes for sugar and beverages. OUR HOME-GROWN FRUITS SHOULD HAVE THE PREFERENCE, *e.g.* apples, pears, plums, blackberries.

The chief nutritive constituent is carbohydrate, and three-quarters of the carbohydrates consist of forms of sugar, the remainder being vegetable gums; it is due to these latter that the making of fruit jellies is possible. The mineral constituents are of great value; they chiefly consist of potash combined with various acids, *e.g.* tartaric acid, citric acid, and malic acid. The general effect of the mineral constituents is to render the blood more alkaline. Fruits used for flavouring are of value in assisting and stimulating digestion.

When fruits are cooked, their cellulose is more digestible; but there is always a loss of nutritive constituents unless the juices are eaten with the fruit (*e.g.* in stewed fruits).

APPLES contain 1 per cent of acids, chiefly malic acid; in this respect they form a strong contrast to PEARS which contain 7 per cent of sugar.

PLUMS contain 1 per cent of protein, which is a high proportion for fresh fruits. They are poor in sugar. APRICOTS, however, have nearly 9 per cent.

CHERRIES contain 10 per cent of sugar.

CURRANTS (WHITE) contain about 6¼ per cent of sugar.

GOOSEBERRIES contain 1½ per cent of acids.

TOMATOES are botanically a fruit, though popularly designated a vegetable.

The following sea-borne fruits may be noted, although they are only occasionally obtainable:

LEMONS are rather richer in protein than ORANGES. In sugar percentage lemons stand to oranges almost exactly as plums to apricots.

BANANAS are amongst the most nutritious of fruits.

FRUIT-SUGAR occurs in most fruits, hence the importance of sweet fruits in supplying sugar as a food-substance.

HONEY is a mixture of grape-sugar and fruit-sugar, and therefore is invert sugar; the flavour is derived from substances obtained from the flowers.

DRIED FRUITS, *e.g.* raisins, currants, dates, prunes, and figs, besides their nutritive value, deserve special mention here as sugar-substitutes in puddings, etc. The carbohydrate present is almost entirely sugar (glucoses).

DRIED FIGS are more nutritious than bread; they contain about 50 per cent of sugar and are the richest in protein of the above-named fruits, raisins coming next.

VEGETABLES FOR EXHIBITION

To grow vegetables for exhibition to compete for prizes special conditions and superior skill are necessary to obtain the best possible results. Its educative effect is great, as the grower becomes more and more intent on learning all there is to be known about the nature of soils, the values of manures, and all the other factors which influence the growth of plants.

Select positions in the garden should be reserved for the purpose, so that it will be possible to give the special treatment required to ensure success. The beginner may not have sufficient confidence in his knowledge of his crops and their requirements, and will probably desire to grow a considerable quantity of each, so that he may have plenty to select his exhibits from; but, as he gains more experience, he will find that with a smaller number of plants he will be able to give them more attention and get much better results. Sometimes the gardener who exhibits at vegetable shows, cultivates the whole of his crops as well as possible, and then makes a selection for the show; but, when this is done, he may have to hold up all his crops until after the selection is made.

The Potato.—The object to aim at in growing Potatoes for exhibition is to secure tubers with shallow eyes, clear skin, and of fair size. A class for heaviest tubers is sometimes included in the schedule of the show, when size alone counts; but as such large tubers are frequently very coarse, this class should not be encouraged. The best varieties only should be grown for exhibition purposes. The tubers should be carefully selected, and placed in boxes for sprouting in the ordinary way.

Planting.—A compost should be prepared as follows: 5 parts of chopped loam (turf, which has lain for a year to rot), 1 part leafmould (decayed leaves), 1 part well-rotted horse manure, 1 part wood ashes, a little sand, a 6-inch potful of bone meal per barrow-load of the compost.

Turn the compost two or three times to mix it thoroughly.

The ground having been well cultivated, make deep drills, 3 feet apart, and place two bucketfuls of the compost at intervals of 2 to 3 feet apart in the drills. Place a tuber in the centre of each small mound of the compost, and pull up the soil on each side of the mounds, leaving the ground in ridges. As soon as the plants appear above the soil, the surface should be broken up with the hoe to destroy the weeds, and to aerate the soil. The usual precautions should be taken against attacks of disease.

Good exhibition varieties are: Edzell Blue, Arran Comrade, Ally, White City, Kerr's Pink, Majestic, and Golden Wonder.

Artichokes (Jerusalem).—The tubers should be of medium size, unbranched, and clear skinned.

Any ordinary garden soil will grow Artichokes. As soon as the soil is sufficiently dry in March, the tubers should be planted singly 18 inches apart, in rows 3 feet apart.

No further attention is necessary until the tubers are ready for lifting.

Varieties: Sutton's White, Sutton's Rose.

Artichokes (Globe).—Large flower heads, well-shaped, with fleshy, well-closed scales.

The soil must be light and well drained, and it should be trenched and well manured in the autumn. In April or May strong, well-rooted suckers should be obtained and planted in clumps of three, 3 feet apart. Give plenty of water throughout the season. When the flower heads are forming, give occasional supplies of dilute liquid manure. To obtain the finest specimens, allow one head only on each plant.

In November, place rough straw manure round the plants to protect them from frost.

Varieties: Green Globe, Purple Globe.

Carrots.—These, for exhibition, should be fine-coloured, well-shaped roots. The

VEGETABLES FOR EXHIBITION

best seed is that which has been saved from the finest selected roots. The soil should be well and deeply cultivated, especially for the long varieties. Sow the seeds in rows 15 inches apart. Holes 3 feet deep should be made with a crowbar for the long varieties, and 1 foot deep for the short varieties, 6 to 9 inches apart. A compost should be made up as follows: 3 parts sifted loam, 1 part leaf-mould, 1 part wood ashes, ½ part of sand, a very small amount of well-rotted manure.

These should be well mixed, and the holes then filled with the compost; leave for twenty-four hours to settle down, and sow three or four seeds in the top of each hole, and covering with an inch of the compost. Care should be taken to prevent the carrot fly from attacking the roots.

Varieties: Champion Scarlet Horn, Sutton's Early Gem, Selected Intermediate, Selected Altringham.

Beetroot.—Quality rather than size is required in exhibition Beetroot. The flesh should be dark in colour and free from stringiness; they should be of good shape, dark in colour, and not have many rootlets.

Sow the seeds in a compost similar to that used for exhibition Carrots in rows 18 inches apart. Holes should be made with a crowbar, 2 feet deep, and 9 inches apart, and filled with the compost. Three or four seeds should be sown in the centre of the top of each hole, and covered with 1½ inches of the compost. When the plants are about 1½ inches high they should be thinned, leaving in each hole the plant with the finest and darkest coloured foliage, as this indicates the finer quality of root. Care should be taken to prevent attacks of the leaf miner.

Varieties: Dobbie's Selected Purple, Sutton's Blood Red, Selected Globe.

Parsnips.—Size and form of root are the objects to be aimed at in exhibition Parsnips. They require as long a season as possible to complete their growth. In the north on heavy soil, it is difficult to get the ground in the proper condition early enough to ensure a long season of growth. To overcome this to some extent, the soil should be cultivated deeply and thrown up roughly 18 inches to 2 feet above the level of the surrounding soil; this will enable it to become warmed and to dry up sooner. The seed should be sown in rows 18 inches apart, and holes made 3 feet deep and 9 inches apart; make up the compost as for Carrots, but it should include 1 part of well-rotted horse manure. Fill the holes, leaving the soil to settle for twenty-four hours, and then sow three or four seeds in the centre of the top of each hole, and cover with 1½ inches of the compost. Thin out the plants when they are about 1½ inches high, leaving the largest nearest the centre of the hole. Prevent the rust disease or leaf miner from attacking the crop.

Varieties: Dobbie's Selected, Tender and True.

Turnips.—Medium-sized roots of good shape and colour, and with solid crisp and juicy flesh, are desired in exhibition Turnips. To obtain these, the time of sowing must be carefully chosen (according to the district). Early varieties, such as Snowball, take from six weeks on light soil to eight weeks on heavy soil. Later varieties, such as Golden Ball, take from eight weeks on light soils to ten weeks on heavy soils to develop. The soil should be well cultivated, and fairly heavily manured. The time of sowing must be carefully chosen, according to the date of the show, the soil (heavy or light), the district (early or late), and the variety to be grown. Prevent attacks of insect pests and disease.

Varieties: Dobbie's Selected Model White, Sutton's Early Snowball, Selected Golden Ball, Selected Red Globe.

Cabbages.—Medium size (except for heaviest Cabbage class), firm heart, and freshness in appearance are the principal points to aim at. The soil should be well cultivated and heavily manured. The seed may be sown in July or August, or in March or April, and the seedlings planted in March and in June. The soil should be trodden firmly along the line before planting, to induce slow growth and the formation of a solid heart. On light soil a mulching of 3 inches of rotted manure keeps it cool and moist, and ensures continuous healthy growth.

Precautions must be taken against insect pests and disease.

Varieties: Sutton's All Heart, Improved Winningstadt, Selected Drumhead, Selected Red.

Savoys.—The cultural directions for these are the same as for Cabbages.

Varieties: Selected Green Curled, Perfection, Selected Drumhead.

Brussels Sprouts.—Straight stems and abundance of medium-sized firm Sprouts are the points desired in Brussels Sprouts. General cultivation as for Cabbage. To

VEGETABLES FOR EXHIBITION

afford the plants plenty of room to develop, set them 3 feet apart each way.

Varieties: Dobbie's Selected, Sutton's Exhibition.

Kale.—General cultivation as for Cabbage. Large plants with well-balanced growth of leaves, finely curled, and crisp to the touch are needed. The centre of the plant must be well filled with young, finely curled leaves.

Variety: Dobbie's Victoria.

Cauliflowers. — Good form, compact heads, pure white, and of fair size are the qualities required in exhibition cauliflowers. The heads will not remain in good condition for many days, hence sowing the seed and planting must be carefully timed, to secure perfect heads for a certain date. The time required for cauliflowers to reach maturity varies with the nature of the soil, and with the season. From four and a half to five months for early varieties, and from five to six months for later varieties. A second sowing should be made a fortnight later. The soil must be thoroughly and deeply cultivated and heavily manured.

The seed may be sown in a flower-pot in February (late varieties) and outside in April for early varieties, transplanting being done in May and June. Early varieties should be planted 2 feet apart each way, late varieties 2 feet 6 inches apart each way. Throw out " blind " seedlings. On light soils a good mulching of rotted manure should be given if the weather is dry, to ensure continuous and succulent growth. In sunny weather the leaves should be doubled over the heads, to prevent their turning yellow by exposure. A good soaking of liquid manure may be given once a fortnight if the soil is light or poor.

Varieties: Sutton's Magnum Bonum, Sutton's Early Giant, Dobbie's Excelsior, Sutton's Autumn Mammoth, Veitch's Autumn Giant.

Asparagus.—The qualities required in exhibition Asparagus are thick, succulent stems, with short, closed scales.

A rich, well-drained, and deeply cultivated soil is necessary. To start a new bed, the ground should be prepared in autumn by trenching the soil to 3 feet deep, adding manure between each spit of soil; the surface may be left in ridges, rough throughout the winter. Planting should be done the following April, setting strong seedlings a foot apart in rows, allowing 18 inches between the rows. Another way is to plant in single rows 2 feet apart, and 18 inches between the plants in the rows.

No stems should be removed before the third year after planting. The soil should meanwhile be kept in good tilth and free from weeds. If the beds are top dressed with cow manure each year and occasionally watered with liquid manure, the plants will become strong and produce good supplies of fat stems for years.

Cutting may begin each year as soon as the young shoots appear above the ground. No cutting should be done after the middle of June.

The finest Asparagus is obtained from comparatively young crowns, therefore where this vegetable is required for exhibition purposes a new plantation should be made periodically.

Varieties: Sutton's Perfection, Sutton's Giant French.

Peas.—This excellent vegetable requires careful treatment to get it in perfect condition for a show on a fixed date. Large pods, fresh and well filled with large peas of good colour and of fine flavour, are to be aimed at. Peas do not remain in good condition long; hence the time of sowing must be carefully considered. It takes about four months from the time of sowing for the pods to mature; but this varies according to the season and the situation. An excellent compost for exhibition peas is as follows: 6 parts chopped loam, 1 part leaf-mould, 1 part wood ashes, 1 part well-rotted horse manure, a 6-inch potful of bone meal per barrow-load of the compost.

These should be thoroughly mixed and then placed in trenches 1 foot deep.

A flat drill 3 inches deep should then be drawn in the compost, the seeds placed 4 inches apart each way over the bottom of the broad drill, and covered with 3 inches of the compost. Staking should be attended to in time to prevent the plants getting twisted or broken, which would check their growth.

When the plants have produced three or four pairs of pods, some of which will be at the proper stage of development at the show time, the tops may be nipped out, thus encouraging the pods already formed to develop to their full extent. If the first pods formed are too early, they may be removed as soon as they are ready for use; this will help the development of those which are left.

VEGETABLES FOR EXHIBITION

This may seem wasteful, but, though there will be fewer pods, each will be filled with large Peas.

Varieties: Duchess of York, Prizewinner, Dobbie's Selected Alderman, The V.C., Peerless, Sutton's Exhibition.

Broad Beans.—Large, shapely pods, well filled with large and tender Beans, are desired. The time of sowing must be carefully chosen. It takes about five months for the Beans to develop to the proper stage. The soil should be well dug and manured, and a dressing given of superphosphate, 4 lb. per pole, and of sulphate of potash, 1½ lb. per pole. Sow the seed in double rows 1 foot apart, and alternately. Give a good mulching of fresh manure before dry weather sets in, to keep the plants growing and to ensure the production of large pods; this also helps to keep off the attack of black fly.

Varieties: Mammoth Longpod, Exhibition Longpod, Giant Windsor, Selected Broad Windsor.

French Beans.—Long, crisp pods of good shape are to be aimed at.

The time of sowing to get the crop in condition at the proper time is specially necessary. The crop takes from three to four months to come to proper condition. The soil must be well cultivated, moderately manured, and dressed with 5 lb. of superphosphate and 1½ lb. of sulphate of potash per pole.

The seed should be sown, two together, in drills 18 inches apart, and 1 foot between the pairs of seed in the drills, one plant being removed if both grow. A mulching of rotted manure should be given if the soil is light.

Varieties: Magnum Bonum, Selected Canadian Wonder.

Runner Beans.—Long, straight, well-formed pods, crisp and fleshy, are the chief points to be aimed at. A compost should be made up as follows: 6 parts chopped loam, 1 part leaf-mould, 1 part wood ashes, 1 part well-decayed horse manure, a 6-inch potful of bone meal per barrow-load of the compost. A trench 18 inches deep should then be made. Break up the soil in the bottom of the trench, and fill it with the compost. The time of sowing should be chosen so as to have pods in the proper condition at the time of the show. Sow in double rows, 1 foot between, and the seeds 1 foot apart in the rows, and cover with 3 inches of compost.

It takes about four months for this crop to develop.

Staking.—As soon as the plants are up, a single bamboo stake should be fixed beside each plant, leaving 8 to 9 feet above the ground. Cross the opposite pieces of stakes at the top, and lay one along between the crossed upright ones, tying each pair to the one lying along the top. This will prevent the stakes and plants being blown about by the wind. In hot seasons, and on light soils, a mulching of rough manure should be given.

Varieties: Champion Scarlet Runner, Prizewinner, Best of All.

Tomato.—Fruit of medium size with clear, smooth skin, and firm flesh are required for exhibition.

Sow the seed in February in a compost of 2 parts of sifted loam, 1 part leaf-mould, and a little sand, and place in a temperature of 60°. When the little plants have made two rough leaves, pot them singly in 3-inch pots, using a similar compost, and place on a shelf near the glass. They may either remain in these pots until ready for potting into large pots, or planting in a border, or they may be allowed another shift into 6-inch pots. Do not plant young Tomatoes in a rich compost, as it causes rank growth. If intended to fruit in pots, the plants should be potted again into 12-inch pots, which should be well drained; using a mixture of 6 parts fibrous loam, 1 part leaf-mould, 1 part well-rotted manure, a good sprinkling of wood ashes and sand, with a 5-inch potful of bone meal to each bushel of soil. When potting, it is advisable to only half fill the pots with soil, the other part being added when the plants have made considerable growth. The soil must be made firm with a potting stick. When watering the plants, give enough water to thoroughly saturate the whole of the soil. When a few trusses of fruit have set on each plant, liquid manure may be given freely to assist in swelling the fruit. All side shoots must be removed as they appear.

Plants grown in the borders in a greenhouse should be planted 2 feet apart in the row and 2 feet between the rows. The soil must not be too rich; but at planting time a top dressing of 3 ounces of super-phosphate and 1½ ounces of sulphate of potash per square yard should be raked into it. Careful watering is necessary. A fortnight or so before the show, the finest fruits should be selected, and if they are shaded with leaves

VEGETABLES FOR EXHIBITION

remove them, to ensure the fruits being well matured and uniformly coloured. Defoliation should not be carried to excess, as it prevents proper ripening and reduces greatly the quality of the fruit.

Varieties: Sutton's Best of All, Kerr's Excelsior, Bountiful.

Cucumber.—Young tender fruits, uniform in thickness, dark green, and short-necked, are desired for exhibition.

The finest fruits are obtained from young plants which are in fruit when about three months old. Sow the seed singly in thumb pots in fibrous loam, in a house with a temperature of 70°. Repot into 5-inch pots before the plants become pot bound.

For greenhouse culture use a compost of 4 parts fibrous loam, 1 part fibrous peat, and 1 part well-rotted manure. Place about a bushel of the compost on slate staging immediately over the hot-water pipes, and put a plant in the centre of each mound, allowing about 3 feet between the plants. Keep the temperature of the house at 70°, rising to 80° on bright days. Syringe the house morning and afternoon. As the young roots appear on the surface of the soil, add more of the same compost until the bed is level. Give plenty of water at the root as it is required.

A stake should be placed against each plant, and the main shoot tied to this. As soon as the leader reaches above the wires of the house, the top should be pinched out to induce the formation of laterals. When the fruit appears, the top of the shoot should be pinched out one joint above the fruit; when the fruit will swell rapidly, and another shoot will be produced from the axile of the leaf. This in turn will produce a fruit; the point of this shoot should again be pinched out as before. In this way fruit will be formed in succession for a considerable period. Superfluous shoots should be pinched out to prevent overcrowding, and if too many fruits are formed some of them should be removed. When the plants are bearing freely, liquid manure must be given frequently.

Frame Culture.—Make a hotbed of fresh, strawy horse manure and partially decayed leaves, building it up into a square heap and placing a frame on the top of it. Tread the bed firmly to ensure slow fermentation and the production of continuous heat over a long period. Cover the surface with 6 inches of soil, to prevent the ammonia which will be given off scorching the plants.

Place about a bushel of the same compost as advised for greenhouse culture in the centre of the frame, or in the centre of each light of a larger frame, and place a plant in the centre of each.

The frame should be damped down morning and early afternoon every day. Air must be admitted cautiously in the early season, and the frame must always be closed early in the afternoon to conserve the sun-heat.

The further treatment of the plants may be carried out as advised for greenhouse Cucumbers. Pinch out the point of the main shoot to produce laterals, pinching the laterals at a leaf past the fruit, and removing superfluous laterals and fruits to prevent overcrowding and overcropping. More soil may be added to the mound as required, and liquid manure given as the fruit begins to grow.

Cucumber fruits grown in a frame are apt to curl; to prevent this a narrow box without ends or top should be placed below the most promising fruits; this will cause them to grow quite straight.

Varieties: Sutton's A1, Austin's Improved Telegraph.

Vegetable Marrows.—Fruits of medium size, uniform in shape, fresh, and tender are preferred for exhibition.

Sow the seed in March singly in thumb pots in loam, and place in gentle bottom-heat. When the plants have made considerable growth, repot into 4-inch pots, and gradually harden them off for planting out in May or June on mounds of fresh horse manure, trodden down firm and topped with 6 inches of loamy soil. Two plants may be set on each mound. A handlight should be placed over the plants during cold nights for some time after planting. Plenty of water must be given during dry weather.

No pinching or training is necessary for Vegetable Marrows, but, as the date of the show approaches, a few of the most suitable fruits should be selected, and some of the others removed to ensure the finest specimens being obtained at the time of the show.

Varieties: Sutton's Vegetable Marrow, Sutton's Perfection.

Egg Plant.—This plant is not commonly cultivated in this country, but is extensively grown in France and Italy. It is grown for its fine ornamental fruits, which are used as a vegetable.

Perfect shape and bright colour are the qualities aimed at for exhibition.

Seed should be sown in February in a compost of 3 parts loam, 1 part leaf-mould, ½ part well-rotted manure, and a sprinkling of sand, in a temperature of 65°. As soon as the plants are large enough they should be set singly in 4-inch pots, and later into 8-inch pots. Water freely, and when the fruit is forming give liquid manure.

If grown for exhibition, each plant should carry only one fruit, but it is usual to allow four fruits on each plant.

Varieties: Sutton's Long Purple, New York Purple, White.

Onions. — Large solid bulbs of good shape, with thin neck and clear skin, are the chief points in exhibition Onions.

The soil must be as deeply cultivated as its depth will allow. If possible it should be trenched three spits deep; but the subsoil must on no account be brought to the surface. Manure heavily with well-rotted farmyard manure, placing a good layer between every two spits as the soil is trenched. A good sprinkling of soot should be raked into the soil also before planting. The seed should be sown in the first week in January to give the plants as long a season as possible before the time of the show. A suitable compost is as follows: 3 parts sifted loam, 1 part leaf-mould, a little well-rotted manure, a sprinkling of sand.

Use 6-inch pots and fill to within 1 inch of the top with the compost; sow the seed thinly and cover lightly. Place a piece of glass over, and a piece of paper on the glass to prevent excessive evaporation. Put the pots in a warm greenhouse or on a hotbed. Lift the glass and wipe the moisture off it every night. As soon as the little plants appear above the soil, the glass and paper may be removed, and the pots placed as near the glass of the roof of the greenhouse or frame as possible. When the second leaf is about ½ inch long, the plants should be shaken out of the compost, and pricked off into boxes in rows 2 inches apart, and 2 inches between the plants in the rows. The compost for the boxes may be similar to that for the seed pots, adding 1 part of well-rotted manure. Place the boxes in the greenhouse or hotbed again. As the weather improves the plants should be gradually hardened off, until, by the beginning or middle of April, they should be hardy enough to be placed outside in a position protected from cold winds by a wall or hedge.

Preparing and Planting the Bed.—This should be done from the middle to the end of April.

If the soil has been left rough it should be levelled, and sprinkled with soot and raked over, making it very firm by treading, and again raking it over. The seedlings should be planted in rows 1 foot apart, and 1 foot apart in the rows.

When planting make a good deep hole with the trowel, to allow the roots to be put in quite straight, the base of the plant to be about ¼ inch below the surface of the soil. When they have made some growth, the soil round them may be removed with the finger, to allow the bulbs to expand freely. Feed with liquid manure once a fortnight, or two or three top dressings of 1 lb. of nitrate of soda or sulphate of ammonia may be applied throughout the season. A top dressing of super-phosphate may be given early in June. The soil should be frequently stirred with the hoe. Prevent the attacks of the onion fly. (See article in Vol. III.)

Feeding should stop by the middle of July (except for the heaviest onions) and the bulbs be allowed to ripen. Twist the necks and lay them over, in the first or second week in August. The plants should be loosened in the soil a fortnight before the show, and a week after loosening they may be lifted and turned over to thoroughly ripen. If the weather is showery they should be placed in a frame, or under cover, fully exposed to the sun.

Varieties: Selected Ailsa Craig, Cranston's Excelsior, Golden Globe, Sutton's A1.

Shallots.—When Shallots are exhibited in clusters, these should be formed of ripe, firm cloves or bulbs. If exhibited singly, the cloves should be large and have clear skins.

A medium soil, fairly richly manured, is suitable for Shallots. Towards the end of February the cloves should be planted singly 6 inches apart, in rows 1 foot apart. These will form large clusters by autumn. In each case the cloves should be set firmly in the soil with their tips just showing. When the foliage turns yellow, the bulbs should be lifted, thoroughly ripened in the sun, and then stored in a frost-proof shed.

Varieties: (Large) Sutton's Giant, Large Red Selected.

Leeks.—Exhibition Leeks should be uniform in thickness, and clear in skin, with

VEGETABLES FOR EXHIBITION

a long blanched neck. They take from eight to nine months to complete their development. Seed should be sown in the first week in January, in a flower-pot or box, and treated in the same way as advised for Onions. When the seedlings have formed a second leaf, shake them out of the soil and pot them up singly into 3-inch pots, and return them to the greenhouse or hotbed, gradually hardening them off until, by the middle of April, they should be ready for planting out. For this a trench, 2 feet deep and 18 inches wide, should be dug, and a layer, a foot thick, of fresh horse manure placed in the bottom of it, treading it fairly firmly; this should be covered with 8 or 9 inches of good loamy soil mixed with well-rotted manure. Set out the plants 1 foot apart. The fresh horse manure in the bottom of the trench will ferment and give off considerable heat, and this will start the plants quickly into growth. It will have decayed by the time the roots grow down into it, and they will thus get plenty of food.

Blanching.—As soon as the plants are high enough, strips of stout brown paper 3 or 4 inches broad should be wound round each plant two or three times and tied round the middle. When the growing centre of the plants is well above the paper collars, the collars should be drawn up, and leaf-mould or soil placed inside the boards round the plants. The collars should be drawn up as the centre of the plants grow above them, and more leaf-mould or soil placed round the necks. As the plants grow in thickness wider collars must be put on. The collars must extend only a little above the growing centre of the plants. Blanching should be done gradually, so as to allow the plants to grow in thickness. When they have become well established, liquid manure should be given once a week, weak at first, stronger as growth proceeds. Liquid manure is obtained from the farm, or by placing ½ bushel of poultry or cow manure in a barrel and filling it up with water, stirring it round, and allowing the sediment to settle before the liquid is used. If boards and leaf-mould are not available, ordinary garden soil may be placed round the base of the plants as the paper collars are pulled up. Two-inch drainpipes should be placed upright between the plants in the row as the soil is built up, and liquid manure is applied by pouring it down the drain-pipes. Five stout canes should be put in at each end of the row of Leeks, sloping outwards, and two or three lines of stout cord stretched along each side of the row. The leaves should then be tied loosely to prevent their being blown about and broken by the wind. It is not advisable to blanch Leeks too quickly or to carry on blanching too long. Allow the plants to grow in thickness as they grow in length; and when they have been blanched to 12 or 14 inches, encourage them to develop in thickness. It is better to have a fairly thick Leek with 12 to 14 inches blanched than to have, say, 16 inches blanched with less thickness.

Varieties: Dobbie's International Prize, Sutton's Prizetaker.

Celery.—Celery requires to have large, shapely heads, well blanched, the leaf stalks fleshy and solid. It takes seven to eight months to grow into first-class " sticks ". Seed should be sown in a shallow box in February, using the same compost, and treating it in the same way as advised for Onions. Never allow the soil in which Celery is growing to become dry, or many of the plants will run to seed. When the young plants have formed a leaf after the seed leaves, they should be pricked out into boxes (using a similar compost to that advised for pricking out Onions) in rows 2 inches apart, and 2 inches between the plants in the row; place the boxes again in a warm part of the greenhouse or hotbed, and when the plants have made some growth, air should be admitted freely, gradually hardening the plants, until by the middle of May they may be placed outside in the boxes. As the plants become well rooted, plenty of water must be given. Planting out should not be done before the end of May.

Dig out a trench as advised for Leeks, and put in 1 foot of fresh horse manure. Tread this down, and cover with 6 inches of good loamy soil mixed with well-rotted farmyard manure.

Place a single row of plants in the centre of the trench, 1 foot apart, and give a good watering after planting. The heat rising from the fermenting horse manure will cause the plants to start with vigour. Liquid manure should be given once a week after the plants have become established. It should be weak at first, stronger as the plants get older.

Blanching,—Exhibition Celery should be blanched by wrapping brown paper round the plants. By this method the plants may be examined from time to time, as new

VEGETABLES FOR EXHIBITION

papers are put on, and the blanched part will be pure and clean.

When the plants have made considerable growth, and the growing centre is 3 or 4 inches high, the plants should be gone over, and all the short leaves and any side shoots, which may have formed round the base of the plants, removed. Strips of brown paper 4 to 6 inches broad should be wrapped round them, firmly but not tightly, and tied near the top and bottom. When the plants grow above the paper collars, broader ones should be substituted, but care must be taken not to use too deep collars, which would shut out air and light from the foliage.

It is not advisable to hurry the blanching, nor to carry it on too long. As in Leeks, the plants should be allowed to grow in thickness as they grow in length.

Each time the paper collars are removed, the plants should be carefully examined for earwigs, slugs, or other pests. A look out should also be kept throughout the season for the leaf miner.

Varieties: Dobbie's Selected Red, Sutton's Superb Pink, Invincible White.

Spinach.—This vegetable is grown for its fleshy leaves. For exhibition purposes the leaves should be large, thick, and dark-green.

A medium soil is suitable, and it should be deeply cultivated and heavily manured.

The first sowing may be made in February, and repeated fortnightly as long as desired. Sow the seed roughly, an inch apart, in drills 1 inch deep and 18 inches apart. When the seedlings are about 2 inches high, they should be thinned out to 2 or 3 inches apart, for exhibition purposes to 6 inches apart, to give the plants room to develop.

When Spinach is required for a certain date, two sowings should be made. If the weather is warm, the first sowing may be too early, but the second sowing may provide the finest plants. If it is cold, the first sowing may produce the best plants.

Varieties: Victoria, Improved Round, Sutton's Long-standing Round.

Parsley.—Exhibition Parsley should be finely curled and firm to the touch.

The soil should be well cultivated, and fairly well manured. The seed should be sown thinly in a flower-pot, using the same compost as advised for exhibition Onions. Place the pot in a warm part of the greenhouse or hotbed. As soon as the little plants appear above the soil, place the pot as near the glass of the greenhouse or frame as possible, to ensure sturdy growth. When they have formed the first true Parsley leaf, they should be potted singly in small pots and returned to the greenhouse or hotbed; later they may be transferred to a cold frame, and by the end of April removed from the frame to the open ground. They should be fit to be planted out in May, in rows 18 inches apart.

The centres of the plants should be well filled with big, nicely-curled leaves, giving a full and rounded appearance.

Sometimes a fine plant may not be well filled in the centre; this may be remedied by fixing a good big pane of glass about 3 or 4 inches above the plant on four small pegs. The glass will draw up the centre leaves.

Varieties: Dobbie's Exhibition, Austin's West of Scotland Prize.

Lettuces.—Firm hearts, tender and of good size, are the points of exhibition Lettuces. The soil should be well cultivated, and heavily manured with farmyard manure. The time of sowing is important, as the plants do not remain in good condition long after the proper stage is reached. It takes from ten to twelve weeks from the time of sowing until the plants are full grown. As the period will vary with the season, a second sowing is advisable. Sow the seeds, three or four together, at intervals of 9 inches in drills, which should be 15 inches apart and 1 inch deep. When the plants are 1 inch high, they should be thinned, leaving the best plant of each clump to develop. If the season is dry, and especially in light soils, a mulching of well-rotted manure should be given; this induces rapid growth and the formation of hearts of crisp leaves. If the Cos varieties do not turn in, they may be tied.

Varieties: Cos — Sutton's Mammoth White, Sutton's Peerless, Dobbie's Exhibition Cos, Austin's Mammoth White; Cabbage—Dobbie's Exhibition Cabbage, Sutton's Ideal, Dobbie's Lemon Queen, Sutton's Matchless.

Endive.—Large hearts, well blanched and crisp, are essential in exhibition Endive. They grow best on a light soil, heavily manured and deeply dug.

Sow the seeds, three or four together at intervals of 12 inches, in drills 15 inches apart, and treat as advised for Lettuces. They take from twelve to fourteen weeks to reach maturity.

To blanch them, cover with large flower-

VEGETABLES FOR EXHIBITION

pots with a piece of stone placed over the hole on the top of the upturned pot, or with boxes a fortnight before the show.

Varieties: Curled—Sutton's Exquisite Curled; Round-leaved—Veitch's Improved Round-leaved.

Radish.—Young tender roots of medium size and bright colour are desirable for exhibition.

The soil should be light, rich, and deeply cultivated, and successional sowings be made every fortnight. A warm sunny border is best for spring sowings, but in summer a cool, partially shaded position should be selected.

The seed should be sown thinly, and the plants afterwards thinned to about an inch apart. Plenty of water is necessary to ensure solid, tender roots.

For an early spring crop, use a hotbed of fresh horse manure, covered with about 4 inches of soil, and sow the seed broadcast on this. In cold weather the frame should be covered with a mat.

Varieties: Olive—Sutton's Early Rose, French Breakfast; Turnip-shaped—Sparkler, Sutton's Red White-tipped; Long—The Sutton Radish, Long Scarlet.

PREPARATION OF PRODUCE FOR SHOWING

For show purposes it is not enough to grow fine specimens of vegetables; it is essential to know how to prepare them and set them out, in order that their good qualities may be seen to advantage. They must be harvested and handled with the greatest care, and each kind must be treated in the special way required.

Potatoes.—In lifting, the fork must not be allowed to touch the tubers. It should be used merely to loosen the soil, and the Potatoes should then be lifted by hand and carefully washed.

Carrots.—A trench, deep enough to reach the tips of the roots, is dug parallel to the row, and a few inches from it. The earth is carefully removed, and the plant can then be lifted without fear of injuring the tip. The leaves are cut off from 1½ to 2 inches above the crown, and the roots carefully washed so that the tender skin is not broken.

Beetroot.—This should be lifted in the same manner as Carrots. The leaves are cut off 2 inches above the crown, which must not be injured or it will bleed. The roots are carefully washed, and the small fibrous roots neatly cut off.

Parsnips.—Parsnips should be dug up in the same way as Carrots. The leaves should be cut off 2 inches above the crown. The roots should then be washed, care being taken not to injure the skin.

Turnips should be pulled up carefully to keep the tap-root intact; they should be washed clean. The leaves should be cut off close to the crown without injuring it. The tap-root must not be removed or injured.

Cabbages with firm hearts should be chosen. They should be cut carefully with all the outside leaves intact. None of these should be removed, and the greatest care should be taken not to break them, or to rub off the "bloom" which covers the leaves of well-grown Cabbages.

Savoys should be prepared in the same way as Cabbages.

Brussels Sprouts.—For exhibition on the stalk, select straight stems, well covered with medium-sized, close, fine Sprouts. The stems should be cut as low as possible, and the leaves should be cut off close in to the Sprouts, so as to show them to the best advantage. If the Sprouts are to be shown off the stems, good-sized, firm Sprouts should be selected, and any small loose leaves round the base removed, leaving the Sprouts quite clean and solid.

Kale are always shown as heads. Plants with finely-curled leaves, and full in the centre, should be chosen; they should be cut low down, care being taken not to injure any of the leaves. Leaves which are beginning to turn yellow should be removed.

Cauliflower.—Well-formed, close, pure white heads should be selected. They should be cut low down, and the leaves cut off level with the top of curd so as to form a green collar round it; any small green leaves which are curving over the curd should be removed to expose its form.

Peas.—Large, well-filled pods should be selected, and the greatest care should be taken in picking them. They are best cut off with a pair of scissors, leaving the stalk attached to the pod. By taking this precaution, the "bloom" will not be rubbed off the pods.

Broad Beans.—Large, finely-shaped, well-filled pods should be chosen. They should be carefully handled so as not to injure them or to rub off the bloom.

French Beans.—Long, finely-shaped pods should be chosen. They must be just fully grown, but still crisp and brittle. One or two may be tested, to see which pods are in the best condition for picking. They should be carefully handled.

Runner Beans.—These should be treated in the same way as French Beans.

Onions exhibited for quality must be thoroughly ripened. They should be well shaped, with thin necks. The roots should be removed close to the base of the bulb, and the top cut off about 2 inches above the bulb. Any loose membranous scales may be removed, but on no account must any of the thick scales be taken off, as the bulbs would then be spoiled, from an exhibition point of view. If the bulbs have been well ripened, the skin should be clean and firm when the loose scales are removed. Heavy Onions should be allowed to grow until the morning of the show. The roots only should be cut off, and the bulbs carefully washed, removing only those leaves which have ripened and would spoil the appearance of the exhibit.

Leeks.—Large straight Leeks, without any bulbous swelling at the base, should be preferred. Dig them up with care, so as not to injure the long leaves or the blanched portion or stem. The roots should be cut off about 2 inches from the base of the plant. There should be no need to remove any of the leaves. The plants should then be washed. A piece of raffia should be tied round the base of the leaves, at the top of the blanched portion, to keep them together. A strand run across between the leaves will prevent the raffia from slipping down.

Celery.—Large, well-blanched, clean heads should be chosen. The plants should be carefully examined to see that they have not begun to "bolt". This can be done by separating the leaf-stalks slightly so as not to break them. The centre should be made up of young leaf-stalks. If it is a solid round stem, the plant has begun to form the flower stem, and must be discarded. The leaf-stalks should be tied firmly just under the green leaves, the roots cut off, cutting into the root-stock by downward cuts, leaving it cone shaped, and then carefully washed.

Parsley.—The plants must be well formed, full, and very finely curled. Lift them on the morning of the show with a good ball of soil attached to the roots; it may be reduced carefully to fit the pot. A 6- to 8-inch pot should be selected, according to the size of the plant or the requirement of the show. The plant should then be potted, and well watered, the foliage being sprinkled to keep it fresh. Care should be taken not to break any of the leaves.

Lettuce.—Large plants with firm hearts should be pulled up, without injuring the outside leaves. Remove only those leaves which have begun to turn yellow, leaving the large healthy outside leaves attached to the plants. Wash the soil from the roots, but leave them on the plant.

CPSIA information can be obtained at www.ICGtesting.com
Printed in the USA
BVOW08s1727261113

337350BV00001BA/63/P